An Evening's Entertainment

By William I. Elliott

Level 4 Press, Inc.
ISBN: 978-1-933769-47-9

Acknowledgements

The poems in this volume were first published in *A Book of Shadows, After the Mallard Sinks, A Plain Squall, Approach, Bitterroot, Epos, Hubbub, Kanto Gakuin University Kiyo, Linews, McMinnville New-Register, Nagasaki, Poet, Poet News, Poetry Kanto, Printed Matter, Psychopoetica, San-shu, South Coast Poetry Journal, The Christian Century, The Plaza* and *Words in Edgewise.*

Tonight's Program

Puzzle Poem

(I.M. Jack Housley)

The last piece of the puzzle
Has fallen into place, thumbed
Into the one
Spot remaining—
The oddest piece of the lot,
The oddest piece of the oddest puzzle;
This piece a part of its sum, the puzzle undone
Until this piece has been placed.

And placed, all pieces in place,
It remains a puzzle,
This puzzle being, in pieces,
Or all pieces placed,
But a puzzle:
Undoing
Into done.

Overture

Bogdan Zabko Potopavitch

A man I'd imagined
Imagined a novel
He intended to write.

He was Estonian
(or called himself so—
Estonia was extant).

Brown knee-socks disappeared
Up sagging gray knickers.
Dark brown cap; smelly pipe.

I unfortunately
Did not know his language.
I had imagined him,

How he looked, what he aimed
To do, but that is all.
Lacking his language, I

Couldn't talk to him, could
Not enquire, fathom, plumb.
On the road where we met

Head-on he smiled, vaguely,
Through his teeth, through a mask
Of smoke; and he nodded.

Twenty steps down the road
I looked back and saw that
We had nothing to say.

An Open And Closed Case

Though we have never seen between the pages
Of a closed book, reason indicates that,
Shut out, light leaves words in utter darkness.
Let in, light, like nothing else, illuminates.

Non-Functional Analysis

Those who run around in circles
Run around in circles
Because they cannot run around in squares.

Love affairs that are triangular
Are triangular
But never isosceles.

Parallelograms are para-
Doxically paral
Lelograms, para
Doxically
Because
Four sides are parallel
But only in pairs,
The same as squares.

A pentagram is possible to write
In iambs and in decasyllables:
Iambic pentagon pentameter

Did Noah's ark describe an arc?
Was it a C he circumnavigated,
His crafty argument half-circular?
And what would logarithm be?
The rhythm of a willow tree in air?
Did Ahab log a rhythm out at sea?
A rhythm out of roots, some cubed, some square?

Meaning

Like every ovum every word
Awaits the one fertilizing
Penetrating spermatozoon
That will release the world in a word.

World, in a word, contained. And now
Sprouting inside the skin of words
I ply to work my way outside,
Break out of the silence of my world

And mean something. Perceive, then,
Edges of the words extruded
Here on this printed white paper
As I poke to puncture our thick skin.

For we are not, until we mean.

Inexperience

The mountains have never stood in order.
They have petrified at a moment's notice
Like cottontails, and when no one was looking
Run like hell. And the sky is also mum,
But seen beneath the obscene sextant wriggles
Like a biological specimen.

The land lies stiff and formal, blending
Into itself as in fear of predators;
And the sky screams inaudibly through the scoop
Of every small boy's manhandled net.

This is to tease us in our brutality;
That if we watch the lashes closely
We shall be embarrassed by the twitch
Of the whole Earth in heat at our cold feet.

A Sonnet In Honor Of Holes

"An empty space in something solid" is a hole
And a hole is always whole. No one ever
Heard of a third of a hole, a fourth, a fifth.
At all events, as fundamental as a myth,
Holes are far more basic than the wheel;
Absences, of which if there were none
They'd need inventing by some clever
Chap. ('Invent' a hole? Can that be done?)

All holes fulfilled, the bottom would fall out :
Keyhole and lock. donuts, nares, the art
Of Henry Moore, the blown or punctured tire,
The hole-in-one to which golfers aspire.
. . . .
(The missing line's a hole for you to fill.)

Theatrical Etiquette

Any more than you would
Five nashi
In a wicker basket

Or the basket empty

You come to No
Prepared not
To applaud gods.

Act One

Adjacent

Standing, at first erect,
Two yellow dahlias lent
A table grace; till bent
With blooming, the table
Flecked with shaken decay,
Nothing remained except
To put the vase away.

We are a standing still
Life, stooping and bereft,
Draped in draining yellow,
Shedding our regalia
And left to lingering.
We are adjacent; and
Still life seems forever.

From Bottom To Top

(For Ryuko)

You could say capricious Fate came round
And wound a top, and spun it spinning
On the floor and O how it whistled C,
High C, at the top of its dizzy voice!

You could say, so is our life together,
But if you did then you would have to hear
High C whistling down the scale to B,
B-flat, the top a-wobble, staggering,
Until completely out of breath
It toppled, lay lop-
Sided on the floor,
All spin,
Whistle,

> Spent. . . . . .
> So

Say the opposite:
We have not been a top
Wound down; that, run down,
We were rather a top set spinning,
Whistling B, B-sharp, rising on the scale to C,
And higher, whistling at top speed. Motion
And gravity defied, we stood up and spun,
Are spinning spinning spinning
spinning spinning . . . . . .

Pointed Out

For Yumi

A covey of quail
Flushed from my brain
Flutter to new cover
Here in the bramble of a poem,
Pretty well-camouflaged.

That Settles It

After the darkness down under
After the tendrils and shoots
After the Blitzen and Donner
After the ravenous roots

Into the darkness and bole
Into the fibre and vein
Into the knot and the gnarl
Into the pulp and the grain

Out of the sunlight and shower
Out of the twig and the bough
Out of the bud and the flower
Out of the therefore and now

Out of the xylem and phloem
Into the mystery—
After, the praise of the poem:
Love is a family tree.

Hospital

She lay there nine and dead,
And cool of skin, off-white,
As of moonlight spooned out
And washed across her lids,
Her brows, her cheeks. Her eyes—
We never saw her eyes.
They'd drawn the curtains tight
And disappeared within
Without a word.

We stood outside and stared.

Sekihara-Sensei

Four seconds in the falling
From the broken railing
To the pavement patio
Head   first   she fell headfirst
She hit   her life abruptly
Ended.   It was 1980.

Still falling she is falling
Still   plunging down the long years
The falling not yet fatal
Because I cannot bear it
That a woman leaning
On a wrought iron railing
Should so suddenly be dead
Her skull no shattered figment
Of my imagination

Because my words will not permit
My dealing with an accident
So rude so hard so brutal
She goes on falling   falling

What Distance Grew

Above the vacant lot streetlights arranged
The night in floating parallelograms;
Light licked along the wires, our voices
Greeted there and quarreled horizontally
Between embarrassed poles, beyond the lights'
Dominion. Beside a lake, above a hill,
Ravens wrapped their claws around our costly
Quarreling and never knew what distance
Grew within their tight objective grasp.

Nagasaki

A girl was
Suddenly piecemeal,
She and Earth reduced to a rubble
Of pebble and bone,
Puzzled pieces,
Shards of shadow
Recalled,
Remembered on the sky
Freakish and misshapen
In the eye of the horror
Where she spins and spirals,
Brooding over the conscience of mankind.

Chaos Theory

Sparrows explode like split seconds
From a hickory

And minnows spurt like milliseconds
In subaqueous slick.

Minute and minuter scatter together
One at a time.

Nothingness

(for Kiyomi)

Standing amid the pebbles of my mind,
I looked outside
And saw the leaves
Strewn in approximate precision;
But I declined
To stay inside.

Standing in a heap of leaves,
I looked, stood back,
And looked;
And then went back inside
And found the pebbles of my mind
Already raked.

Sitting by the pebbles,
I rose and raked them over
In concentric ovals in approximate precision;
Stood back and looked,
And declined to go outside
To rake the leaves.

Deeper Dark

There is a dark deeper
Than shadows' darkness:
Remember the air
Blanketing the pages
In a closed book, where
Darkness is utter.

The Death Of Imagination

What you see
Who march before they
See who march behind
Who see the street
Is lined not with people;
Unexpectedly
Not lined at all
With people. The whole
Hamlet marches one
Way and only one.
You see no faces
Who see you, who
See you whole, you see
In your periphery
Parts of faces, pro-
File who in
Periphery see
Parts of you and parts
Of those who al-
So march abreast,
March smart one way,
One before, behind.

Case In Point

Drape drawn over the mirror,
The mirror reflects the drape.
This neither elevates
The status of the drape
Nor demeans the mirror.

Act Two

Legacy

Death had a bone or two to pick with her.
Abducted in the dark of winter, she
Met her stalker face-to-face and quickly
Disappeared, spirited off to elsewhere.

Her legacy? An indelible shadow
Floating on the ground before your eyes;
A visage that resembles you and me,
And one that seems to smile.

          Or can that be
The wind, merely, its little wispings
Teasing the dust into mild bemusement?
Wherever I go the shadow follows.

Chameleon

Her shadow lay light on the grass
As of a skin shed;
Something of a piece she had removed
And spread out on the grass
Now gray through the transparency.

When I looked again I saw
Gray double darkening with black,
A black that seemed to float above the grass,
The gray suffused with black,
The black the color of my soul
That could not cast a shadow
And borrowed all of her colors.

Descant Upon A Temporary Stay Of Execution

The institution teems with inmates.
It is nowhere near filled to the gills.
Cells await that can accommodate
Numberless others. Within limits
The incarcerated roam the grounds
At will, though the majority keep
To their dim cells. Awake, I summon
This one or that, for no known reason.

It is when I am asleep that they
Insist on my keeping office hours.
They move in a closed world of shadows,
Sliding in and out, pausing, fleeting.
And all though on death row will not die
Until they die with me, the day I die.

Haunted House

O this house is haunted
And behind the hollow
Walls a *mysterium*
Tremendum rattles lath.
How tentative your path
Is, twilight always spares
You the delirium
Of knowing; on the stairs,
Midway, afraid to swallow,
Where the blood leads, follow.

When you reach a landing
In the rhomboid-above
You will touch in the nil
The boards clawed by the black dove;
And up the stairway still
The trim creature will dive
For another landing,
And you will be standing
In the twilight, alive,
Of, O, this haunted house.

Milkweed

The stalks of milkweed stooping
In a crooked year—
They are but witches turning
Their bitter nipples to bees;
But never suckled,
In a crooked year
And dragging their burred tresses,
Dance dryly, wryly, cackling
The curdled songs of virgins.

Hag

She struck a match to tease a wick,
She hissed out an entire tier
Of votive candles; stood witch
In the strychnine darkness cackling

Least, lost in the star-stack
Flick out Earth in a tick
Of its prime, a brief bead
Nicked in the barter of time.

And out of a hooligan sleeve
I swear four thousand fireflies
Came pelting the smouldering darkness
With elliptic anonymity.

She hailed whores in the star-swarm
On an abacus rosary,
Filled the holy grail with hearsay,
Jammed a needle through a camel's eye.

The Man In The Forest

Haunting, was it not, the hooting?
    Haunting, was it not?
That is why you lost your footing.
    Rest now on the cot.
  Haunting, was it not?

He has drawn the blind, my dearest.
    He has drawn the blind.
What you hear now is the sheerest
    After-play of mind.
  He has drawn the blind.

Do not try to speak—you stutter.
    Do not try to speak.
Sleep alone will be the utter
    Comfort that you seek.
  Do not try to speak.

More than haunting—foul, the note, dear?
    More than haunting—foul?
Sounds that wobble from his throat, dear,
    Simulate the owl?
  More than haunting—foul?

Did they not forewarn you, dearest?
    Did they not forewarn
That a menace in the forest
      Thrived on broth of thorn?
  Did they not forewarn?

It was by the spring he caught you.
 It was by the spring.
It is to his hut he's brought you;
 Dumb, or he would sing.
It was by the spring.

Haunting, was it not, the hooting?
 Haunting, was it not?
That is why you lost your footing.
 Rest now on the cot.
Haunting, was it not?

Repossession

Come upon a palette
In an attic studio:
Abandoned colors coagulate,
Crack in the stratagem dust;

Or come upon the pleat
Of a crumbling wall-ward vine:
Tethers of tendrils ruminate
The contents of dynasty.

Come upon a panoply
Within a dark museum:
Who held the deed to this estate,
Looted all in calm neglect?

Or come upon a plot
Of forsaken monuments:
The unremembered congregate
Beneath forget-me-nots.

The Garden Of Now

I have seen God sigh a monsoon,
Slip from the rim of a light-year
To rapids of stars, and dangle
His feet in the tumble and wake,
And withdraw them dripping the dross
Of fossils of ice turning lake.

I have seen God muscle the strings
Of orbit into mutiny
With a terse baton of lightning;
Heard the eardrum of creation
Burst, plunged in a font of eclipse;
And seen the house of heaven rise
With Author on their crater lips.

I have seen a tattered creature's
Starfish flesh sliced up at wit's end
Into the paradox of life.
I have seen God strike flint on flint
And spark the tinder of spirit
Raging with a yield of light.

I have walked in the Garden of Now
And found it as In the Beginning.

Still Life

It is fitting that three felons are nailed
Against the far wall of the sky, frozen
In the posture of the cruciform;

Fitting that the weary morning world
Should witness the end of a schism
On a hill, slowly; that the taciturn

Sky should collapse in a fragment of fog,
Dropping the impenetrable dregs
Of indifference on the mock-heroics.

Why do mirrors crack and goblets sting?
There holy by the grace of God he hangs.
The morning is meant for hysterics.